CW01508861

QUALITY CONTROL
AT THE MIRACLE FACTORY

First published in 2025 by
The Dedalus Press
13 Moyclare Road
Baldoyle
Dublin D13 K1C2
Ireland

www.dedaluspress.com

ISBN 978-1-915629-40-1 (hardback)
ISBN 978-1-915629-41-8 (paperback)

Dedalus Press titles are available in Ireland
from Argosy Books (www.argosybooks.ie) and in the UK
from Inpress Books (www.inpressbooks.co.uk).
Printed in Ireland by Print Dynamics.

Cover image 'Assemblage No. 5' by Patrick Cotter.
www.patrickcotter.ie

Dedalus Press receives financial assistance from
The Arts Council / An Chomhairle Ealaíon.

QUALITY CONTROL
AT THE MIRACLE FACTORY

PATRICK COTTER

DEDALUS PRESS

ACKNOWLEDGEMENTS

Gratitude to the editors of the following publications where a number of these poems, some in earlier versions, have appeared:

Amphibian (Netherlands): 'Chart Song'; *The Amsterdam Review* (Netherlands): 'Ghost of a Sort,' 'Lives of a Girl'; *Anthropocene:* 'Hats'; *Blackbox Manifold* (UK): 'The Piano'; *Connotation Press, an Online Artifact* (USA): 'Self-Portrait as 21st Century Frankenstein'; *Consequence* (USA): 'Notes of the Court Interpreter'. 'Good Will Recital – Sonata in G Minor'; *Cyphers:* 'Flyfisher'; *Declaimer* (UK)*: 'Wall'; *The Honest Ulsterman:* 'Angels over Nagasaki'; *The Hog River Press* (USA): 'Flesh Boy' *Howl:* 'Child Wake'; *The Lily Poetry Review* (USA): 'On Pruning And Other Matters' 'Like Prisons, Our Own Gifts' *The Manchester Review* (UK): 'Farriery'; *Marrow Magazine* (USA): 'Bird-Catcher', 'Umbels', 'We are Golden' ; *The Irish Times:* 'Self-Portrait as a Silk Purse' 'Levant Diptych'; *Poem Alone:* Pig Factory; *Poetry Ireland Review:* 'Cilice,' 'At War's End,' 'Equine Cinderella'; *Prelude* (USA): 'Cobs'; *The Shop*:* 'Stolen'; *Temenos Academy Review* (UK): 'Self-Portrait at Sixteen'; 'Self-Portrait as Half a Sculpture in the Luxembourg Gardens', *'Unbroken* (USA): 'Crow, My Friend'; *The Waxed Lemon:* 'Husky'; *Windows*:* 'Goat Dreaming'.

*Extinct journals

Contents

1

The Mare I Meet The Week of Your Death / 11
The Child Being Raised By Owls / 12
The Carecrow / 13
Doll Maker / 14
Reverse Mermaid / 15
For What This Row of Rabbit Heads in my Wardrobe? / 16
Filial Duty / 17
The Ringmaster's Complaint / 18
Serenader / 19
Rehearsal / 20
Weather / 21
After the Hurricane / 22
Springtime Gift / 23
Elegy for a Corkwoman Who Died in Winter / 24

SONGS IN A TIME OF WAR

Babushka / 27
Chart Song / 28
At the Munitions Maker / 29
Louse Float Daze / 30
Spilt Milk / 31
A Conscript's First Kill / 32
Raider / 33
Good-Will Recital – Sonata in G Minor / 34
Angels over Nagasaki / 35
Generation Shift 1967 / 37
Wall / 38

Psalm / 39
Levant Diptych / 40
Notes of the Court Interpreter / 41
Gaza Fugue / 42
At War's End / 44

WOE MENAGERIE

Snail Notes / 47
Crow, My Friend / 48
A Horse Called Franzine Marc / 49
Equine Cinderella / 51
Hats / 53
Pig Factory / 55
Goat Dreaming / 57
Farriery / 58
Cobs / 59
Husky / 60
Moths / 61

from THE LEE ROAD CODEX

On Pruning and other Matters / 65
The Piano / 66
Scenes from the Lives of a Girl / 68
Flesh Boy / 70
Umbels / 72
Like Prisons, Our Own Gifts / 73
Bird Catcher / 74
We Are Golden / 75
Losing Face / 76
Flyfisher / 78
Cilice / 79

THE STATE OF THE BLESSED DEAD

Regrets / 83
Child Wake / 85
For a Living Wage / 86
Coffin / 87
Ghost of a Sort / 88
Stolen / 89
Three Months Later / 91
from The State of the Blessed Dead / 92
Self-portrait as a Silk Purse / 94
Self-portrait as 21st Century Frankenstein / 95
Self-portrait as Half a Sculpture in the Luxembourg Gardens / 97
Self-portrait at Sixteen / 98

NOTES / 100

1

The Mare I Meet The Week of Your Death

i.m. Anna Barden

The dry stone walls are as grey as a lionsteeth clockface
and the long-necked horse, her pelt as grey as the lime-
stoned way to the shingled strand. A breeze blows

to beached-froth her unbraided mane. Tangle of neck
muscles like a moon's eye view of a cyclone's swirl.
Lengthy muzzle hairs prod the air like misplanted

eyelashes. Her prehensile lips form a glove
concealing a hand opening and closing the jaw
full of honed piano keys dicing the flexible green

blades of the roadside tufts, the wall's farside
little Eden, little wilderness, spared till now the mown
fate of the enclosed paddock. Yesterday in the same

field she reared and galloped as if chasing a ghost.
Now she turns an eye the size of an anemone's bright
corona to blaze on me, her low gruff whinnies

like flat stones skipping across the pond of my hearing,
her impatient ear flickering, unpredictable like a moth's
dullest wingbeat – from such fractions of life are sagas seeded.

The Child Being Raised By Owls

She crams the nest as a breathing, sweating
cushion of heated velvet. She coos in the minor
keys of melancholy – echoes of the nightly
mantras of her plate-faced parents, with so much

brain dedicated to so much eye. In starlight
she is myopic by comparison. She will never fledge.
The nest extends like an expanding loaf as she grows.
What she learns is compressed into moss-

upholstered hours. Like a welcomed benign
cuckoo she has perfected the art of being mothered
perpetually. Five broods of siblings have sprung
since her arrival. She had been lifted like a delectable

lamb but chosen to be raised instead of eaten.
The owlets cleaved close to the glowing bars of her limbs
thriving on heat, though her larger mouth caught more
of the shreds of rabbit and mole her parents tore.

The pellets of indigestible pelt she has learned
to chuck up, spreading them about her like a mammalian
mattress. She'll grow and grow until the bough fractures
or until all legendary wisdom pecks its way out of her skull.

The Carecrow

I'm pitched in solitude in this field shaped
as a circle by my creator. Overhead, a globe
of sparrows in flight presents its face of underwings
but flits no closer. Furrows spread as radials
from my feet to the field's circumference, hedged

like a verdigrised metal rim on a beaten cake tin.
Maize fills the furrows with ripening cobs, like poured
custard on a flan of stalks and red soil. My head
is a skull of purged wasp nest, weather-proofed
with pitch. Severed robin wings serve in place

of earlobes. To crows they are the greatest joke
as a would-be killer pulling out, in error, a flimsy
feather instead of a dagger, might be to you,
or even me in the past life I'm not here to speak
of. I was remade to turn a bird's covetous appetite

to leadening stone in his chest, when he nears me,
nears the field, nears its crop. Any bird but a crow.
Upon my face in white paint is a corvidian smirk
only crows can recognise. Ruffle-necked ravens
are rendered uncertain by the dialect of their smile.

All other birds perceive the grimace of an avian
annihilator. Here maize is reared for the benefit
of crows alone, whom my maker loves for their humour,
intelligence, guile. But I, I care, but am not caring.
My smile is not my own and the cackle of crows irks.

Doll Maker

I have composed a bespoke voicebox, inserted not
in her throat but in a cavity where a heart might verb
and reverb. Provoked by tilt, it chants a wail, its timbre

uncanny like the tolls of the local belfry, kindred enough
in song to stir a far-flung emigrant to weep in memory.
Once, a collapsed shelf loaded with such implanted chests

unleashed a squalling chorus of lament in my graveyard-
quiet workshop. She is delft-headed, as if a teapot
had grown a face and shrunk its spout to a pert

bivalve sneeze-vent. She is a whelp of my imagination
and manufacture, fingerling of my wistful musings
and whittlings. Her irises are shaved, green marble

of Connemara. Her hair I've weaved from the seed-
wisps of wild clematis. I have made her for a granddaughter
slumbering in a distant timezone. The future for her

is a different country demanding allegiance to the polythene brats
of mass production, to bawl in a different accent, to know
nothing of the keening century her *seanaithir* first inhaled.

Reverse Mermaid

I have the gilled neck, the finned, scaled torso of a benthal
native, with the hips and legs my sisters so often long for.
I'm wounded by the impairment of tailless propulsion

through the sea's saliferous liquor. When I tire of swimming
I amble along the sands of the shallows, careful my mouth
never rises above the billowing surface to sputter on air.

Over the earth's face I am less than a barnacle on a whale's flank.
My delicate feet dodge the shearing shivs and shanks
of limpets and whelks, the lassoing flex and flux of kelp

and dulse. The depths furnish me shelter from the muted
roars of trumpeting tempests. There the ghosts of so
many spent clouds and glaciers glower. My posing sisters

prefer the plinths of shoreline rocks and to frolic
in the termini of estuarial funeral marches, to anoint
themselves with the sweet sweat of distant mountains

poisonous to my tongue. A lunar clock times my own
sardic effusions, a monthly lure for the ravenous sharks
and orcas I have so far outswum, with cunning not speed.

For What This Row of Rabbit Heads
in my Wardrobe?

My forming face was embossed in the womb
with the crudest die, asymmetrical, stippled.
And as a green child I was subject to the creaturely
gawking of my peers, wild and unschemed. As I grew,
in me the urge to meld unseeable with the earth

grew too. But no flesh is forged to fuse or melt without
burning, rather just to be and to shift about like a leaning
spire of blatant meat. Not for me the proudful pose
of the handsome with the double prow of that chin
and nose shearing through the air as he struts towards

the vales of satisfaction. I have learnt to mask all year
round, to assume a semblance of avatar more prevalent
in the byted ether. Here in the proddable universe,
not even outside Halloween or inside the wrong Chinese
year do people care anymore. For me the daily question,

which rabbit face do I don today? All are white with eyes
pink, arranged like a display of fedoras, bred from giants,
large enough to squat on a human's adult shoulders.
Hollowed out for the world not of holograms.
Which nose will do my snuffling today? What whiskers

to carry out my careful navigation as if they can scramble
the way like yolks? Each eyelash is cosmetisised
with a glebe of ersatz tear. My hand does the choosing
without the guidance of my arm, like the blade of a spade
whose staff has reverted to unforming molecules.

Filial Duty

As a willing boy I stepped into the thicketed forest,
into its cathedral-tall marquee of chlorophyll. Light
leached away from me as the present receded and a shifting

path beneath my feet whisked me along like a departing
hearse, below a chorus of breeze-voiced leaves, their smooth
sirenaic whispering. Coils of briary bramble struck out

with a thorny scorn I evaded. No sconcing satnav
scouted ahead. I had only a needling instinct to guide
the way, past atramentous berries with their tart aroma

of fermenting bellies. My haversack of bequests was light
with devices of dissembling, stacked layers of mâchèd-
paper masks moulded by my mother; left with her letter

of posthumous instruction to dress with them, to drape
a particular tree in these woods, one seemingly dead
of perturbed bark and wretched, shrivelled roots; home

to sprites whose faces are too beautiful for the world to bear.
She wrote: "The masks are so they can stare at us in safety, eyes
saying, *your faces are full of expectation we cannot feed*".

The Ringmaster's Complaint

I juggle butterflies while my hands stay steady.
They dart from palm to palm like tossed clumps

of dried petals after months and months of bile
and terror, I mean trial and error. Leashes

of graphene and fingers soaked in the tears
of buddleia nectaries were key. Flea circus

methodology has been useless, as has training
from the egg with all memory made soup

in the chrysalis. Caterpillars, like lumbering
lumps of sushi with a face, have their own repertoire

of tricks until pupation to the form of a blue whelk
far from the ablutions of the sea. How exasperated

I was on the first opening of the hatchery door.
Eclosions of flying fuschia scattered like flocks

of unherdable thoughts. How was I to make
rhythmic, patterned unity from such fluttering

chaos? Each vacated chrysalis dull as an extinguished
lantern, birther to a multi-dimensional Rorschach test.

This rare and useless art of no rewards obsessed me
until I could be master. And now I await the fritillaries'

ennuied desertion, their ragged flight from the past-
bragging tone-shop of my heart, still pumping.

Serenader

In the laneway, he hugged the voluble headstone of the accordion.
Its ivory keys affecting a stave of vertebrae. Ponderous were his
    fingers
in their choosing, coaxing slow blending chimes, as notes queued
like jostling complaints, building a tune no thrush would filch.

Maybe a cockatoo pitching to mock would echo this dirge as if
she'd swallowed heteroglottal reeds, bellow, grille of the Scandalli
purchased at scandalous cost. The song had been a hit in his youth
when beards were debonair, shaped as if hewn by couturiers.

Two long socks, drying from a fourth-storey window jig to his gig
between linen sheets thwacking like plates of flexible metal.
He recalls a young woman of long, long ago, her gentle melodious
chuckles, how two knee-length socks were sveltened by her feet

and calves, other times, gathered in shapeless folds around ankles –
images mummified in the natron and myrrh of his memory,
memory a tuning fork to every song he will play or hear.
With tendons of iron his fingers and elbows strain out each note

now to sound fluid as tears, as the north wind is sucked in
and compressed over the pliable reeds; crystal seeds of ice banished
by the warmth of the strains, wresting from the weighty box a
    piquant
melancholy, with the socks flapping like flags of insulating
    surrender.

Rehearsal

At eleven, the undertaker's daughter poses in an airy
shroud of black tulle, like an astonished trout-head

in a gagging net. She does not smile. She is grimace-
free. She knows only those with a mouth as rested

as an unread book earn heaven's entry. The mirror's
curtailed universe is her hearse of repose. She sees

she is ready-stilled for the velveteen belly of a casket,
still enough for the servant powers of night to lay claim.

The sacred sack of her corpse feigns readiness to be
consumed by six-foot stygian cliffs on four sides,

for the raining of soil shoved by shovel to fall on her,
gritty with flakes of snail shell, shards of mouse bone,

husks of earwig-deserted chitin. But first, she pauses
to thread her pigtails through the cores of Samhain's

apples and course-tasting cakes of soap, to embalm
the barmbrack's fabled ring, pea, bean, vengeful stick

in her doughy palms; for copper Britannias – opaque
unbrittle spectacles, to seal her eyes; her ginger eyebrows

a raggedy fringe to the lustrous ancient coins.
She awaits her father's black-clad, teenage apprentice,

he of the Maraschino cheeks and grinning eyes,
humming Bauhaus or the Cure or Sisters of Mercy.

Weather

To be from a parish of low hills and stumble-trek
into a kingdom where the greyed skies are impaled
on cold mountains. The corpses of clouds cling
to escarpments as snowpacks ready to calve and stampede
downhill towards the funnelling valley, rushed to sea
so heated and raised again into the nimbussphere,
or not, and left to drift, to disrobe layer by layer, to expose
cadavers centuries old undigested by the earth. I could
pass the savage edges of penitentes razored by the sun
and pass by, further on, a crevasse – a malevolent rictus
eager to gobble my tottering being whole. I would heave
against the wind, made body, with freighted iceflakes
the infill of its shape, walloping my face in waves.
I would be but a mote in the blinded eye of the mountain.

After the Hurricane

My father sought the faded flight path
to our linen and his soul, as if any mistral
or zephyr would have magicked him
to that place. Since the linen soared off
we've scoured our faces with sheets of steak
sequinned with clots, fetid with blood's density.

The linen took off in the storm – unsequenced
squadrons of warped rectangles defying gravity.
As cold and wet prattled to our exposed ears,
lightning, thick as an eel, forked down my father's
throat, hooked his soul on its jagged edges, hauled
it away, away with the linen. All week after

stuck in doldrums, he perched on the hillock
of lumber once our house – wings of remongered
umbrella spokes sheathed in cowhide impaled
on his shoulders. He willed a surge of levitation
with all of us hopeless as a stilled windmill, luckless
as hunting cranes in flood-flushed, frondless ponds.

Springtime Gift

In the front living room, rugs of shadow
are rolled up by the sun's advancing reach.
And the struggling flimsy flower rooted
in the broken window flings its colour
at the householder, too depressed winter-
long to deweed the seedling from the sharp-
edged crack in the glassy pane – draughty source
shading her lungs and spirit with brackish
cloak. Now, bold hope stealths to slay its callous
oppressor with scythes of light. A preying
animus, compelled to compress the small
house's core smaller without moving walls,
quivers itself, as it shrinks, powerless.

So sun and hope kick all brute shadows dead.

Elegy for a Corkwoman Who Died in Winter

Forty-year-old waif, wife to the roofless
streets you perished on. My glancing face
as familiar and regular to you as cutting
winds. I was one who gave without ever

giving enough, clawing in the crannies
of my jeans for coins and fluff, silvery
and brassy tokens with the value of old
coppers, poor exchange for your smiles

and thanks. Vanessa, you had a ten-dollar
name living thruppeny bit days. You knew
our gaits, you listened for our tinkling hands
but never knew the inside of our heated homes.

Small comfort now to you the fires of cremation,
our tepid tears as the flesh drifts off your bones
like smoke, when all along your skin deserved
to be lit by pearls, unctioned by L'Oréal and Chanel.

Songs in a Time of War

Babushka

Every May at peak bloom, in her daisy-patterned
dress, arms spread out as if bound by tethers, her body
bait for blessings to cling to, she stands beneath

the shedding cherry blossom, petals falling like slow
trembling shrapnel. Perfume of the flowers thick enough
to catch in the throat. The illusion of time stilled, though

cellular shift is yet ferried by on rafts of nanoseconds –
the creeping attrition of flesh. All her skin sagging,
the developed wrinkles of a century showing in her measled

flecked mirror. Over nine decades her improvised
habit has morphed into ritual, the mumbled prayers of her
own making ossified to liturgy. Wars and putsches entered

and exited her life with the regularity of dance steps.
Beloveds died. The older and the younger, her parents,
her children. Nowadays she rarely sleeps, she has lived

beyond all nightmares, to chant her cant of singular
charm, to stand eyes closed amidst the gathering kirshy
carpet at her feet, free and costless, to remember the dead.

Chart Song

Before the war, the boy who walked only on his hands
could have trod on his feet had he wanted to, but liked
his eyelashes occasionally touching the ground where
he was entertained watching the adventures of ants

capturing long-bodied, long-haired caterpillars, before dragging
them back to their nest for a flossy feast. When the earth
was dank, flocks of snails abounded and their antlers tickled
his nose. He could have confidential chats with his own shadow

speaking right into its ear in whispers heard by no one else
except the worms and the earwigs scuttling beneath leaves.
At home he ate out of a dog bowl on the floor because
his mother indulged him. When he slept at night he hung

loose as an empty noose, upside down, from the attic rafters.
His mother told everyone he was home-schooled, claimed
he was so intelligent because more blood flowed to his brain.
All this stopped the day he had no body to cry next to, only

the offal stains on the pavement where his father stood
when the spray of shrapnel shred him. Before the war
whenever he whinged his father would stoop down low,
put his face up close and say "Where did you learn that song?

That's a great song. That should be in the charts. That's one
of the greatest songs I've ever heard." And the boy's whine
would segue straight into laughter. For after all what did he
really have to cry about before his father died in the war?

At the Munitions Maker

Like a spread of giant nits, howitzer shells
stand stored in ranks on the factory floor,
flat ends down, the point where a louse breaks
loose aimed at the innocent ceiling. Each stout
putative bomb awaits its slicks of paint to mark
maturity, to be owned whole by defining livery
as if all day long distant enemies can care how
death is dressed. See now how a moron's *bon mot*
is calligraphed on one side, while, on the testing range
amidst the blast-stirred dirt ragged shrapnel lies sown
like chopped-up ploughs. There, a fragment outlined
like Donetsk, another is cookie-cut to seem the Azov
Sea frozen, as if steel could creatively visualise, manifest
alone the world's bloody destruction into being.

Louse Float Daze

après Ashbury

Your vague republic's military uses my nation's
landmass like some emerald traffic aisle. We
could lobotomise about this for centuries or watch

endless replays of Helen Topping Miller's self-
regarding vlogs. So I cradle this average anthology
that showcases only forgotten villanelles while some-

where echoes a dull de-training. I hear of a place
where – after your dream stitching's last bombthru –
the climate was still floral and all the wallpaper

in a million homes stood exposed by fallen brickwork.
Thus I'm left gobbling thornapples by daylight
arranged in nocturnal coils as the hobnails of your

happy-go-berserky zouaves go stomping by.
The different weights encapsulize a scholarly
setting down as the singer thinks in progressive stages

like a skyscraper. Bisque figures in cerise and cornflower
blue turn a slightly grotesque silhouette and prisms
clarion alarum in an old army blanket.

Spilt Milk

The blood, at first fountaining
then merely oozing from the sniper's
slack-heaped victim, pools like mercury
into a looking-glass puddle. The surface
coagulates like skin on cooling custard.
Its reflective metallic finish fades fast.
Zoom out to a great distance and it is
a fractal of an inland sea shrinking
elsewhere on the planet's surface. Iron
in the haemoglobin creeping preferentially
towards magnetic North, no longer
an expression of the body whose spleen
forged it. At day's end it will be
a lickable snack for a neighbourhood cat.

A Conscript's First Kill

The water tepid now but the village aflame.
A bath drawn, unused. No rim of floated filth,
discarded skin, no suddy, lacy overcloth tabled-
down. My steel-toed boot to its metallic pod

sends ripples scudding the surface, disrupting
gravity's still command. And again with a mortar
shell's nearby impact; kick-up of earth a fallout
showering short of the water. The liquid still pure

yet too undersanctified to scour sin from my hands
or the Halloween gore forming my naked mark's
shroud. Adrenalin still heaves my breath as my soul
drags itself from a berserker's crisp chrysalis.

Raider

The marram grass reaper dressed like an elite
trooper. Beret, charcoal fatigues, boots Dubbin-
waxed. As if the stiff stalks compelled an approach
with stealth. During the war he was a Commando
risking execution on every landing in France,

his face buffeted pitch to blend with night's
inky cover. So now, each trip to the beach
was devised as a mission of hazard. He advanced
on the grass with such aware intent he could grab
by hand nesting plover, but plover were not his quarry.

He sliced marram with the swiftness a jugular demanded
when the tufty blossom had wilted and ripening seed heads
started to warble ragged lullabies amidst the wide coast's galey
howls, outsinging his earworm of Rhineboys' throat-cut gurgling.

Good-Will Recital – Sonata in G Minor

The young soldier who plays the cello is kitted
out for his levelling-of-civilisation day-job.
A pixelated camouflage haversack beside him.

His chromed assault rifle almost wistful in its
leaning. After he has shown mastery of Chopin
he must leave to rubblise still-rollicking streets

where musical notation, the craft of luthierie
are yet nurtured. He sits and plays and fails to notice
loose linden leaves crushed beneath his buffed boots:

perfect practice for his hobnailed soles.
Their percussive potential as they crush, almost
an intended duet with a rifle's life-quenching sputter.

Angels over Nagasaki

"Although the majority of Americans may be Protestants,
they are still Christians, which means that both the assailants
and victims pray to the same God."
-—Shōmei Tōmatsu

"Gallagher, who flew in the B-29 which dropped the A-bomb over
Nagasaki, said his brother found it in rubble after the war and gave
it to him as a memento."
—Union of Catholic Asian News

After the bomb, a cemetery of angels
a flightless bevy – just heads and wings

silicate heavy – Catholic gargoyles
with wavy long hair and long faces

with aquiline noses, none boxed flat
by *Fat Man*, its plutonium fission,

its esurient airburst over a tennis court –
love-forty-thousand, with a morel cloud

as score-keeping umpire and a Charles
Sweeney as mad as any Sweeney, mad

all his life with no mercy for Sunday
wafer-swallowing women, children,

old men, none of whom had banzaid
at sorrowful Nanking or Pearl Harbour.

A mad Sweeney with no need for a yew tree
to hoist him into darkness, to help him incinerate

innocents for his God-trusting Protestant
republic. Even to begin with, the angels,

they had no eyes, no pupils at least, no
mirrors to their souls, no eyelashes to shed

after fallout, no business for Rimmel
or Maybelline, but still they could witness

faces melt from the heads of the faithful.
And for years they lay in their graveyard,

scrabby grass struggling to stretch up between;
waiting for a cathedral to resurrect, while,

actually, one did lose face, was effaced –
a sacrifice in solidarity with the losers

of flesh, a left cheek all that remained
after the Protestant Republic's merciless

flypast, picaroon-crewed half by Tadhgs,
a Gallagher as well as Sweeney. One angel

was lifted as a trophy, like a Byzantine lion
pillaged by Venetian louts, contrabanded

to Chicago. After forty years of fermenting
remorse, Gallagher dispatched her back,

all five compact kilograms of her,
with a Jesuit for a guardian and apologist.

Generation Shift 1967

The child's fringe had jagged gaps as if
his mother was drunk when she set at him
with the clothescutting crimping scissors

or as if his head never rested as he struggled
to resist his locks' shorning. *Clip. Clip.*
They lived in a remote coastal village

aeons and vowel-shifts as wide as a continent
from Carnaby Street and its sharp-clad habitués.
They lived where no discos, no galleries, no men's

shirts with floral patterns were to be found.
But still the village boys yearned for locks
brushing their collars, locks at odds most possible

with the shaven heads of their forefathers
whose palms still burned where the King's shilling
had sucked at their souls, who feared unkempt hair

was the work of despair overcoming them, the despair
comporting with night visions of long-dead boy-comrades
screaming for their mothers, others, arm outstretched, rasping

'Help me'.

Wall

Here in the square is the sole spot the barber
can scissor under shade. He snips the boy's
locks, facing the wall flecked by bullet pocks

and specked by blood, scorched-umber-mottling
staining the wall, till next it rains. The boy's hair
falls in clumps of black cloud on scrabbling ants.

Sweating candle stubs and wilted flowers rim
the brick base where last All Souls Day stood
skulls weaved from bleached chicken bones,

skulls with polished nuts for eyeballs – AMOR spelt
across each forehead in twisted wishbone fragments.
The army hasn't soldiered through town for weeks.

No widows have been recently made. The boy's
brain melds a menagerie from the patterns
of bullet holes and blood on the wall: a vulture

spreads its wings to flee a viper's uncoiling interest;
a jaguar licks its chops as it pounces on a peccary.
So much swift death on this wall.

Psalm

The headless Christ of Nagasaki blesses the faithful,
his corpus a short-term sanctuary for the souls unhoused

by their bodies' atom-struck evaporation. Radiant sacred heart
on his chest like a flaming grenade. *Fat Man* beheaded him,

chipped at the cuffs of his tunic's stone sleeves, snapped off fingers
of one hand at the knuckle. Suffered and wounded like the actual

Christ, he's now a better avatar for prayers than the sculptor's
pristine creation. Across the city a clutter of dissection tools

on a cadaver's chest is like an upturned drawer of cutlery.
Out of the depths of its stomach's cavity, out of a *Geistlos*

cul-de-sac, like the well of an uncured leather boot I'm unready
to try on for size, crawls the gleam of light which had toppled in.

Levant Diptych

i Who Needs A Burning Bush?

For sidelock ringlets are like the script
of God, vowel-free, ready to drip
onto the scrolling page right-to-left
and at the barber shop, as their trimmings
fall to the floor, they spell out the name
of the latest child to be bulldozed
homeless, not far enough from Nazareth.

ii October 2023

The shellshocked donkey is mantled with dust
except where rivulets of blood channel down
from his headwound. He cannot hear bleating
from his own mouth, a pitch and rhythm
not unlike the siren of an antique ambulance.
He's not standing. He doesn't know
if his legs work. Collapsed buildings
pile around him in asymmetrical lumps.
Metres under his belly, crunching in the dark,
Gaza's last apple for miles has been put in the mouth
of a child hostage to keep her from screaming.

Notes of the Court Interpreter

for Damir Šodan

In the video of evidence Coca-Cola
received free product placement.
Its realness and thingness extolled,
as in a crisp philosophical treatise behind
the darkened face of the suffering woman.
In tabloid reproduction, the white script
on crimson background was excised.
A witness testified the killers left in a black
Lada sedan, its tyre marks slicing a cursive
swathe through the molten, oft-churned peat.
In the distance, on the horizon, dogs, birds
were mere diacritic marks against the dusklight.

Gaza Fugue

after Paul Celan

Grey rubble of twilight we claw at you in the evenings
we claw at you at noon and in the morning we claw at you at night
we claw and we claw
a man lives in a bunker he fiddles with markers on a map
he writes when darkness comes to Judeah your golden hair
    Shulamith
he writes and paces around his room while his jet engines flare
    in the sky
he trumpets his Merkavas out, a crater is gouged from the earth
he commands us head to the North

Grey rubble of twilight we claw at you in the evenings
we claw at you at noon and in the morning we claw at you at night
we claw and we claw
a man dwells in a bunker he fiddles with markers on a map
he writes when darkness comes to Judeah your golden hair
    Shulamith
your ashen hair Nayrouz, a crater is gouged from the earth

He cries haul your jumble to the North, you others just bleed
he pats his Merkava on the turret, he sets it off roaring
haul harder your jumble to the South, you others just bleed

Grey rubble of twilight we claw at you in the evenings
we claw at you at noon and in the morning we claw at you at night
we claw and we claw
a man dwells in a bunker your golden hair Shulamith
your ashen hair Nayrouz he fiddles with markers on a map

He cantorises haul harder yourselves to the West
a Merkava is an angel of Judeah he shouts haul harder your carcasses
there will be a crater gouged from the earth, in there you can bleed

Grey rubble of twilight we claw at you in the evenings
we claw at you at noon and in the morning we claw at you at night
we claw and we claw
a Merkava is an angel of Judeah, her flag is blue
she shells you with incendiaries her aim is true
a man dwells in a bunker your golden hair Shulamith
his jet engines flare in the sky a crater is gouged from the earth
he fiddles with markers on a map and dreams a Merkava is an angel

your golden hair Shulamith
your ashen hair Nayrouz

At War's End

In place of a machine-gun tripod I plant
an artist's easel, targeting the same ground.
While I sketch, my simpleton brother prances
across the scene, starkly threadless, bodyhair

alone keeps the sun's full glare from his skin.
The star's welcome strafing reddens him
by the minute, while leaving his blood's
full flow coursing inside. He channels

a gazelle's soul as he leaps against
the horizon, maimed aspen treelets
framing him on either side. His hands
imitate horns as well as forelimbs.

His fingers spread too apart to be mistaken
for hooves, even on my canvass. He leaps
and leaps with a regularity he will never
have the energy for again, as when

the next war ends, after shuffling through
the old streets where all we can recognise
is the cobblestones. Meanwhile I smoke
to give shape to the devils infesting my mouth.

When I exhale, *you* can witness their forms,
sinuous and snakelike as in all the best bible
stories, even those where they remain
unseen, unpainted, like when Jericho falls.

Woe Menagerie

Snail Notes

Whorley snail, terrifier in its botanical realm,
ravager of leaves with its shearing jellied
mouth. Its shell protects only against shrivelling
desiccation in a drought. It scabs a snotty screen
across its home's gaping floor. A shrew's milk teeth
could crush the crisp of its armour. As a baby, poised
on a daffodil stalk, it is a mobile brown globule
slowly pouring itself, a muddy raindrop, an uphill-drip.
Sometimes slow enough to appear still, like an inedible
stone or flake of wind-dropped bark to a cloud-high
crow. For all its ponderous existence it extols no
philosophies, but provokes thought in others, not least
tulips who rasp at one another through their roots
at times of ooze and prowl, after dews and wind howl.

Crow, My Friend

The crow I knew well enough to receive presents from, shrugged with ennui at the neighbours' sonic traps. Unconvincing mechanical broadcasts of crowhen caws in breeding season. The neighbours hated his moulted feathers, raged at his cynical shitting on their backyard. His guano was fuelled by the nuts and cat kibble I fed him by the trowelful. We knew they planned an endgame with crushed plumage and bloodied guts. They never had their win. I fed him for the presents of crazed creativity he airdropped: the feathered fish-hook like a damselfly, the platinum screw from an aristo's sit-in trainset, the brass clasp from a child's Chinese casket. I could go on. The cat could not compete with the gist of these gifts. Dead mice and sparrows, old bones, the sort of present the cat herself would like to receive, littered my doorstep to no avail. The crow delivered treasures he had no use for. No twigs or worms, snails or berries; he devised presents from crafty observations of my likings. He grasped the manipulative genius of empathy. This went on for more years than I thought a crow could live. Over time we swapped our songs between exchanges of food and trinkets. I read to him from Mahon's *The Hunt by Night*. He garbled a huge range of ticks and caws, burbling and cooing, expounding his mysterious corvid dialectics with a satisfaction as if he believed I understood. It couldn't last forever. The winter he disappeared he left me a letter in the shallow snow. Claw prints, in patterns as complex as avian cuneiform. I failed to photograph it before the thaw.

A Horse Called Franzine Marc

The horse who savoured art favoured the textured
surfaces of oils, their tangle of pigments, the palette
knife's signature scrawl, but wasn't adverse to figurative
sculpture. I first met that horse standing by the side

of the street waiting to be talked to. Truly, as a stranger,
to converse with a horse one must sit on one's haunches
and wear a black homburg. And if the horse is interested
in your story she will lower her head, moving her feet

as little as possible lest the clip-clopping upon the concrete
ground block out any of the words you have to share,
especially words of praise about her braided mane, intricate
patterns on her coloured blanket and her tail arranged

like a bouquet of orchids. I was to learn all this
was a mark of her dedication to the life of an aesthete.
She would sneak, as well as a tall looming beast
could, into the National Gallery, iron shoes pocking

on the marble hallways and staircases. Unusually for a horse
she had zilch interest in equestrian subjects and knew enough
about Duchamp and Beuys to be unembarrassed when
she dropped, with tail raised, an ephemeral treasure,

fluffy and fragrant. An arts journalist could not cease
speculating if this was meant as guerrilla art
or critical commentary. The National Gallery blocked
her entry after warning letters from their insurance

broker. When they couldn't source a rodeo star
to guard the entrance they hired a matador. When
that didn't work, a lion tamer. Some snobs presumed her
to be one of those underprivileged equines from the suburbs

used to living in a high-rise flat, until one day they witnessed
as she crossed the Liffey by the Ha'penny Bridge,
her break into the Lipizzaner prance of one well-travelled.
Impounding might have been her fate except she never

crossed roads without waiting for the green man. At the Douglas
Hyde Frida Kahlo retrospective, nobody was surprised to see
    Robert
Ballagh aloft on her back, with all the confidence of long
companionship, conversing, agreeing with her approving neighing.

Equine Cinderella

I've squandered summer after summer wandering from strange vale
to strange vale, mart town to mart town, holy-grailling after
the horse
whose foot could cover the shoe thrown through my window
one wet

night in November nineteen ninety-three. A shoe three hands wide
with nine big holes for nails. It looked like it could only have shod
a horse of war. Huge enough to fit as a torc around the thick

neck of a champion ram, a hackney or thoroughbred's skittish hoof
could step into the middle of this shoe and leave space for a broad
corona between footprint and the shoe's inner rim. I've been
searching

so long now the horse must long be dead, burnt on a pyre or
minced
for pet food, but still I hope its progeny stamps somewhere. An
Ulster
blacksmith regaled me with his father's mythologising of
horses with such

legendary feet, but he had never seen one himself. He said the
weeping fields
of Agincourt sick them up, such mystery shoes, twice a century
at ploughing
time, corroded to red crumbling crisps. Mine was definitely of
more modern

make. When I find the stallion to fit it, I'll sell my cottage of
   turfed roof
and the field beside it brimming with ribbon-winning Kerr's Pinks,
to pay for him. And pass the last of my days making the ground
   shake

with galloping charges, bucket on my head, fireplace poker
   brandished
with my weakened old wrist, skin like onion paper, like the
   agèd skin
of my grandmother I noticed as a boy, her armour of decades
   still resisting.

Hats

The donkey obsessed with hats rooted
himself to the pavement outside Vignoles,
the town milliner, who had adopted
the grape variety name as a *nom de*

plume in recognition of all the wine-
coloured feathers he had imported
from an Oceanic speck noted for its birds
of paradise. The donkey had no particular

interest in feathers, although he welcomed
now and again pigeons alighting on his brow
or between his ears, assuming the role of headcover.
Once, when his turfcart was unloaded

of its haul outside McCooney's Bar
he raced to the town's outskirts, past
the sign saying *Welcome to Ballycarraig*,
onto Jack Kerr's turnip field, dragging

the cart behind as he galloped, ploughing
up the newly broadcast seed with hoof
gashes and wheel ruts, all to reach the scare-
crow at the field's centre, or rather, to grab

with a backlegs-powered leap the hat of straw
atop the crown of the man of straw, he of faded
'70s fashion cast-offs. Previously, the donkey
had been owned by a big-city street performer

who had trained him to climb a step ladder,
to balance on his hind hoofs, with a rugby
ball atop his muzzle, held in place by the nimble
manoeuvrings of his tongue. The donkey knew

the ball was not a hat, but still took note of the smiles
and laughing, the claps and yelling a foreign object
on his head provoked. There was many the goat
trained to do this trick, but he had been the only donkey.

Pig Factory

Among the honking, snorting throng, some child's
pet – a *banbh*, bottled-reared and brow-stroked
whose widening grin and happy waddle
were cuddled until the day came to be prodded

into pork, to be portioned and packaged in the factory
in the city where often a leering Camas moon
arced over the hill. There, a line of clattering
hooves whose honks turned to the squeals

of rusty hinges, hundreds in a chorus.
And the squeals turned to screeches of terror
and the screeches turned to screams of excruciation.
And in the houses next to the factory, people too poor

to move away paid no more heed to the squeals
than they would to the high-pitched chatter
of children in a schoolyard at breaktime.
And the screeches blended in their ears

with the screeches of gulls by the weir
where a culvert spewed into the river bits
and blood the rats and mullet scrambled for, too;
blood beyond the congealing of drisheen,

beyond the Pollack-like streaks on the walls
visible when first-floor doors were ajar on hot
days and the wafting scents of scraps made
the local moggies yawn at their privilege.

All this I know and yet that *banbh* I eat
albeit without its grin and the ears that wiggle
no more, dressing centre-table at the dinner parties
of well-earning, slumming gourmands.

Goat Dreaming

Even the caged, tame goat can dream
of a distant mountain, inclines mauve
from the blossom of heather smelling
sweeter than any bagged feed; memories
of a mountain he has never been near,
moving from gene to gene like the yellow
of an eye or the kink in course white hair.
At the Christmas fete, the cage rests
beneath a flimsy canopy, flaps are steady
in a windless moment, a moment
when the goat is calm from his steady
dreaming, dreaming the thoughts:
"It is the narrowness of the limestone
ledge which keeps me standing
and not a cage too narrow to lie in."
The milling market throng is a bank
of passing cloud, too urban to know
of Puck, too sober to kneel in obeisance
to caprine royalty. For in pagan memory
goats can be kings and vain kings can sprout
ears like goats, though not here in the city's
grey, not here in the Street of the Yellow
Horse, where clouds pass by on feet.

Farriery

He feeds his favourite tree at night
with headlights. The leaves lap up
the Toyota beams. It will flower soon
just for him. His stallion will be garlanded
early. Bridled with blossom of chestnut,
fragrant with sweet scent. The horse's mane
matches his lover's in length and russet hue.
He stares with pursed lips from the parked
Prius, into the night over the beams, as if
into the future when life has settled like a hoof
and the years have already brought all the past can hold.

Cobs

The whippet called cygnet
held its ears flat in an effort
to mimic its master's mood

whose young face had more lines
than a school jotter. His raccoon-
rimmed eyes were like adjacent

water wells with depths never
lit by sun. An airbus flew overhead
coming and going to places the man

had never been. In all his life
he had come no closer to a plane
than to swans in flight, heaving

with effort, with wheezing wings.
It seemed to him the streets
were crowded with mothers

pushing antique, black enamel
prams; their still children looking
like wax mannequins lying in state.

The whippet called cygnet was white
and mute but its snout was not orange,
and the only cobs it knew bristled with corn.

Husky

In the land so featureless everything looked the same,
smelt the same, where the polar bear with cunning
concealed her black nose on the hunt, the otherwise

dark-haired husky had a white head to hide her smile
against the snow. Her master threw more treats
when in a melancholy mood – brain-filled fish-heads,

rainbow-hued offal and the like. She grew sturdier
than her dark-faced brothers and sisters whose happiness
was as evident as their salivating tongues were long.

They had to make do with dried, baby-seal ears
and narwhal jerky. And still they stayed happy.
Their smiles as wide as a Beluga's seemed, as obvious

as the Aurora Borealis. She learnt hiding your happiness
was easier than faking your sadness, even when a master's
melancholy loved company. The white-headed husky

had no words for snow, unlike her master who had dozens
and dozens in degrees of nuance. But she made up for it
with her barks. Even her barks were white and blent with the ice.

Moths

Her ex, the lepidopterist, displayed trophies
of butterflies, squadrons arrayed behind glass
in black frames on his bedroom wall. Their colours
and little faces as lifelike still as when on the wing.

The room was small. The wall was crammed.
Death aestheticised, death collectivised her mantra.
Years later life had space for just one-night stands.
She cast living masks of each of her passing lovers

as they slumbered. None seemed to mind the gallery
of men's and women's faces hung over her bed,
over their heads. None thought to return and find
their own face staring sightless across the room.

Each August, in peak season, she sprayed phero-
mones on her tongue before heading on her night
walk. Giant yellow male silk moths would fly
into the cavern of her mouth looking for love.

The wings tasted dry but the innards were as delectable
as prawn flesh, without tough chitin to cough out.
Sometimes, even after her fill, moths still stumbled
through the night, drawn by her breath until a seething

globe of ever-moving yellow ribbons formed a tight
shroud. If the fluttering had stopped she might have choked.
She could feel with her feet her way home, oblivious
and blind to everyone observing her along the way.

Before entering her house she shook off the moths like a scarf of leaves. She tumbled into sleep under the pupilless eyes of absent, scattered lovers, echoes of wings like silky tinnitus her happy lullaby.

from The Lee Road Codex

On Pruning and other Matters

The man with a tree rising out of his head stopped
feeling guilty for his talent long ago, the gift he'd never
earned, never asked for. The one he was born with.

You believe I'm special, he'd think to himself, *but I'm only
you with my head growing a tree.* People in town squares
would throw coins at him, pin banknotes to his twigs

while he just stood there. During the season his tree fruited
childless women plead with him to fill their wombs, often
holding their husband's hand as they presented their petition.

Does it hurt to have your berries plucked? a boy once enquired.
Only when they're still green. He'd wander from town to town
all through the climate-varied continent, trying to keep one step

ahead of autumn and its leaf-stripping powers. Occasionally
he would seek out a tree-surgeon. Nothing could prevent
pruning from hurting, no drugs, only skill could lessen it.

But without prudent clipping the branches would grow
too large to let him slip through doors or properly rest his head.
Once a bonsai master told him *The things I could do for you*

without ever elaborating. Tree-man scoffed and moved
on to the next town, leaving a pair of sparrows flying overhead
searching for their missing, cheeping nest, bills full of mayflies.

The Piano

Each morning after rush hour they emerged
from a doorway on Cal Teobaldo Power:
the men who could never venture out without
a piano over their heads – a baby grand,

so that it took ten of them to walk all over
town without strain; down by the pier,
where you could swear the seagulls
sang sean-nós between gulps of fishheads;

through the marketplace where aging hippies
flogged courgettes, stained glass earrings
and wall masks fashioned from porous,
crumbly solidified magma; past the 3D,

metre-high, cut-out, white-lettered sign
of the town's name against which tourists
selfied, with the sea and dormant volcanoes
posing behind them. The piano cover, red

velvet, reached down to the waists
of the men so nobody could see their faces
and the piano legs were six feet long
so they could set it down when they reached

a café and order coffees or aperitifs they sipped unseen.
Thunks and clangs fell to their feet whenever they were
on the move. Of course, it was never in tune, and yet once
I heard the first three notes of McCartney's *Yesterday* peal out

perfectly, followed by the right-length pause before more pure cacophony like the arrhythmic pulses of metal-hearted beasts. "If we could all live long enough, and watch them do this billions of times, eventually we would hear *Love is a Many Splendored Bird*

played perfectly by complete accident,' said the man
I later learned the locals called 'Professor'.

I didn't know whether to be happy or sad.

Scenes from the Lives of a Girl

i

The dead leaves clung to the young girl. They leapt
from the earth to clothe her. The linden and the oak,
elm and sycamore. Every time she arrived home she
was met by her exasperated mother moaning about
the leaves' flaky deposits in her hallway, the baby slugs,
the not completely dead aphids. "Why don't you brush
them off before you come home?" Her mother presumed
electricity in some static form had a hand. She never
witnessed the looks of astonishment that greeted her
daughter all along the road as leaves swept themselves up
to envelop her, astonishment too deep to rally an insult
or catcall. Astonishment of a kind no emoji exists for.

ii

When the little terrier snapped and barked, the tenyear-
old girl's hair rose suddenly in a wild thicket over
the top of her head, too plentiful and thread-like
to make her Medusa-like. It was not the first time.
Her hair-burst happened only when no one else
was around. When she was five a jackdaw alighted
on her shoulder and cackled quietly with elongated
gurgles. The sensation had been long known to her
but here for the first time she saw her reflection
as it happened, in the low window of a low sportscar
parked alongside. She knew it was something strange
because if it happened to anyone she knew they never
talked about it, so she resolved neither would she.

68

Long ago she had learnt she couldn't will it to happen,
not even through seeking the company of animals
when alone. Always without warning, three times a year
it occurs, when she has forgotten to expect it. Someday
she hopes she'll understand what it means. If it means.

iii

The daughter of the doll vendor hoped to be
bought herself, to be purchased, put in a box
wrapped with a ribbon, to be carried far
from her mother, from her scathing remarks,
unpredictable clouts. She held her eyes open
as long as she could with a glassy stare, wearing
a dress not too dissimilar to some of the dolls.
Her mother sold mannequins too and dolls of all
sizes. And once she almost got lucky. A cigar-
chomping American tourist enquired after her price.
Many customers almost reached that point
before noticing her exhaling or going puce from not
exhaling. When her mother caught her doing this
the girl was left with a black eye or a bruised
cheek, the easier to distinguish her from the dolls.
Her favourite companion was a store dummy in a top
hat and a wig of long black tresses, like Morticia Adams.
Now that was the kind of mother she could approve of.

Flesh Boy

The boy with ghosts for playmates pondered
if he should die himself. Non-life didn't seem
too wicked, to judge from the tittering of kindergeists.
They never had to fret about a litter of flinty stones

on the ground, rending holes in the knees of their jeans
or the rowdy grousing of an empty stomach breaking
off an interesting game, hurtling them home to eat.
And bullies couldn't lay a finger on them. Dying young.

How else could he hang around to continue playing?
He guessed from his scrutiny of grown-ups
he wouldn't like to clamber up trees all his life
or leap with abandon over permeable skipping ropes

twisted by spectral wrists. He knew his wraithful
friends couldn't grow with him, but he wondered
if he would get to know the spooks of older people
as he aged himself. He quizzed the ghost kids

but they just shot the frozen stare you'd expect
a computer to show if a computer could respond
emotionally to a question it found meaningless.
If he befriended the ghosts of older people

would they want to do boring older people
stuff with him, like sit in the garden for hours
reading magazines and drinking tea or stand
at the sink staring blankly out the window,

sponging dishes, or dabble all day in a tool shed
achieving nothing compelling? He knew
whatever, he would probably end his grey-haired days
with ghosts or spend his everlasting days as a ghost.

Umbels

The boy snares frogs, kisses them, hopes to conjure up
princesses with rippling tresses and fabrics to provoke
him into fathoming what lies beneath. He fastens some
amphibians to a string for days, strokes them, soothes them;

devises a ritual where his feet must be bare as he catches
them with his left hand. None yet mutates, while in his pocket
huddles a stolen nest, an unravelling mess of twigs and mummified
leaves. He waited ages for the eggs to hatch – only one ever did –

a scratchy, scrawny escapee from its splintered cell.
It fluted a never-resting cheep until he found it an ant
and a stream of tattered flies purloined from a spider's web
and earthworms chopped into wriggling bits. He smashed

the unhatched eggs, teenchy as marbles – the stink tear-inducing,
and part-formed embryos lay still in a stew of green. In time
the squeaky cheeps turned to song and pin feathers unfolded
into a blue tit's plumes. When the bird flew away, the boy

resolved he would swear off love and never be a father.
But the clamour of croaks still beckons him on nights
when the wind blows from the east and the lakeside rushes
push out their umbels of blossom, pink-veined, fragrant.

Like Prisons, Our Own Gifts

The boy under whose bed a forest rumbled could not slide
asleep without listening to the mournful hooting of owls,
the howling of wolves – all at such a soft calming volume

since the critters needed to be teeny enough to dwell in a forest
sprouting under a boy's bed, a forest never shedding its leaves
despite the permanent darkness and dearth of rain. In certain

seasons he could thrust his hand inside, and apples the size
of regular apple seed peppered into his palms, tarting his mouth
as any rare variety when chomped by the handful. He kept

the cleanest room of any boy, so his mother had no excuse for
    rushing
in, scouring under his bed, discovering the forest, sweeping it away
with sperm-crusted socks. He never stayed out all night, stayed
    in weekends.

All his nightmares dramatised a forest being scooped up, plopped
in an ash bin; miniature deer, owls, wild pigs and wolves, apple
    trees,
elms, oak, sycamore – all engulfed by the housefire's light,
    sterile leavings;

binmen carting away his world to a putrid landfill to be snaffled
by monstrous rats and ravenous seagulls roaming far from the sea
leaving his underbed a tomb, his soul a derelict site of seclusion.

Bird Catcher

The woman who trained her hair to snare
birds had needed to spool it long and sinewy

like mooring rope. So so long it rolled
below her bum, her knees, her feet, and rolled

metres along the rough grainy ground if
unrestrained. When quiet it gathered

in black coils on her back, nesting there until
an errant blackbird or reckless thrush thrusted

overhead to be speared by the black silky forks
of locked lightning. She avoided bellicose bellowers

like bulky herring gulls and full-grown ravens
on the wing, but swans, geese she could strangle

if ambushed on the ground. She scoffed all flesh
she could, reducing her appetite to pathetic pecks

before hawking the rest to a shabby, contraband butcher.
Robins and delicate wagtails she sautéed and steeped

overnight in sycamore blossom honey for breakfast.
Her favourite season was when swallows measled

the sky and swarms swung within reach of her vehement
strands, Stuka-swooping her as she neared their nests. Puh!

As if she would ever covet eggs. She loathed eggs, their broken
witchy slop raised the skin of her nose and knuckles in goosebumps.

We Are Golden

The girl never went outdoors without a starfish
clinging to her forehead – glued-on rather.
A fresh fumbling aster of the rockpool
needed to be sourced every third day. The one

desiccating, smelling, she fed to the patient cat, so
afterwards, cat's turds made for stinky stardust.
Her father deemed such dismal rigmarole to be
youthful pretension, one she should grow out of,

begging his tolerance and patience meantime.
As a teenager himself, each day, he had renewed
a painted canker on his cheek, a mark of artistic
protest against the surface comfort of everyone

surrounding him in the spiritually-crumbling
city, where mostly those not poor enough to be
forced away, remained. He viewed his daughter's
affectation to be an expression similar to his own,

even if nothing alive had to die to decorate *his* face.
If he hadn't grown out of drawing cankers on his cheek
he would eventually have had tattooed something
permanent, but before that day could arrive he

perceived the invisible, unscourable, metaphorical
canker as indelible as any ink-under-skin on his
and everyone else's face. The whole city had one
except his daughter, who knew starfish fed on them.

Losing Face

The man who lost half his face in the war
still shaved the half he had left. Just because

he had no nose and no lips to cover his teeth
didn't mean he would foreswear looking

respectable. Though he had long ago waived
expectation of love. He had been the son

of a balloon vendor but was never allowed
a balloon himself. He had had nothing but

contempt as a boy for children who craved
balloons, their whines, spoilt dances until

they received what their tantrums commanded.
His greatest, deepest contempt was reserved

for those who cried when their balloon floated
away after slipping from their fingers. His face

was a balloon he refused to weep over even if
he had still been able to shed tears. His father

had been a hunter in his spare time. Over years
had amassed dozens and dozens of skulls of deer

he had shot during the long peace before the war.
The walls of their home bristled with faces of skinless

bone the man thought now were his closest friends.
The twists in the antlers mirrored the bony emotions

churning in his belly. Halloween was his favourite
day. He could strut all over town with a mask of a whole

normal face. People on every street corner would gaze
at him as if they could love whoever was behind the mask.

Flyfisher

The man who snared flies with a fishing rod angled
only indoors. He had the patience of a devout hunter of trout,
casting his lines to the far nooks of a room. Instead of hooks
he used sticky paper, and different coloured gut
for different kinds of fly – common housefly, fruit fly,
bluebottle, midge. The reel he owned was antique and the rod,
bamboo. He swore off non-organic fibreglass with a shudder.
He rented himself for five cents an hour and all the coffee
he could drink. Each fly he caught was placed, minus
its wings, in a matchbox. At day's end he shook
the contents down his throat and intoned a special whisper
to aid digestion. As he worked he always wore a gloss-green
bowler festooned with cobweb, and a frayed-collared tweed jacket.
A twirly-ended moustache rounded off his look.

Cilice

All night he dreamt of purple-tinged clouds. The day following,
to mark independence, he weaved his shirt from thistledown
harvested near sunken headstones in an extinct sect's forgotten

graveyard. He made his fingers raw from the down's extraction;
the scent from his skin coarse from the seeping sap. He disavowed
power-cutters. Only the scythe's rhythmic swish would do:

the semi-circular motion slicing the proud heads from their spines
of nourishing chlorophyll. The heads' flesh he pulped on a replica
Stone of Scone to a green oozing cud good for dying. The fluffy
    down

he rolled and weaved for the silken cloth – white, flecked with
    purple
like the extravagant linen-infused paper of the last Kaiser's deflated
Reichsmarks. He had collected them like stamps as a schoolboy

with the placenames no one learns anymore: Breslau, Königsberg,
Danzig – wiped from the map like a scythed thistle.
The shirt was fine, fine as a Charvet to wear – nothing like horsehair.

The State of the Blessed Dead

Regrets

The woman who awoke in a Hieronymus
Bosch painting couldn't tell which one

not from her perspective. She was naked
not cold, but still compelled to snatch

cabbage leaves to robe herself. On
the horizon, menaced looming pink

follies shaped like body parts she was too
unworldly to recognise. It took her fortnights

to realise she trod through Boschland
foraging on berries, wrasses with wings

and weird feathered vermin like evolutionary
cul de sacs. Even when the pig clad as a nun

snorted past she still could not determine
which painting. The nun, nude of concern,

simply honked when quizzed for directions.
No matter how far the lost woman trekked

the pink stirrers of clouds miraged no closer.
Even from so far away she could see in clarity

they were orbited by a haze of droning creatures
like a murmuration of flies over a corpse. Her

memories were vague with murky scenes
from what seemed an alternate life, where

her eyes stayed closed and blue bottles
harmonised above her and those who loved

her could never edge closer, no matter how far
or hard they scoured the surface of the earth.

Child Wake

For a dead child lying in state there must always
be angels on display. Plaster and wooden figures
procured in haste, venerable with cracks and peeling

paint, in wild contrast to the pristine smoothness
of the corpse's face. Candle-flame quivers in veneration.
Lilies exude their funereal fragrance with a pollen excess

ballooning in a narrow space – no longer toxic to the human
mite without working lungs. A teenage aunt prays
for a miracle, a twitching eyelid, a jerking foot, a chance

for the new white shoes to be scuffed and scraped
rather than sealed with their unworn perfection
inside a coffin to go underground. She knows the gods

will not spare her this indulgence. None of them.
Even though she beseeches each and every one
she has learnt about, from Aten to Odin, Jesus

to Jove, Aphrodite to Buddha, and all the saints,
all the animist receptacles of souls, all of them listening
to her naming them over three long days and nights.

For a Living Wage

The suburban cemetery is another cage failing
to contain. The parakeets break the gravediggers'
picket line, passing overhead in raggedy vectors
with jocular jabber and tropical garniture, affronting

the decorum of grief. Rooks rasp like a spade shivving
clay, a sound cradled by the yew tree's inner ear
in absence of burials. There are no union-busting scabs
among the dead, though obsidian-sparkling hearses

clog the access road like arterial plaque. With engines
idle, the Zyklon-like exhaust fumes have stopped
puttering their smut all over the hedgerows. With all
crematoria combusting from dawn to dawn and booked

out for fortnights, in hospice morgues and funeral home
fridges, coffins are piled like cells from a busted hive,
the corpses within are maggots purloined of wriggle. Past
the strikers a sparrowhawk streaks by like a palling auger.

Coffin

The man who could not afford a grave
carried his baby's coffin everywhere, tied with twine

to his back. It was crafted of good solid pine.
Though the corpse was light he was not unburdened.

It was cumbrous and tight whenever he turned
a trick, the odd labouring job, stacking

lumber, shovelling ditches, hefting bricks, sponging
windows; but needs must to earn to save for his spot

of diggable dirt approved by a priest. A simple
wooden cross, winnowed from landfill would do

to mark it, but the gravediggers union couldn't let him
dig the hole and risk redundancies. He felt guilty

for every morsel he forced between his teeth; its cost nudging
further and further away the day his precious could be buried.

He could afford no coins to place on his baby's eyes
and had instead planned to use bottle caps filched

from a fancy restaurant's wastebin, until one day,
sitting exhausted on a streetcorner, a passerby

mistook him for a beggar and flipped him a copper
farthing of a withdrawn, unspendable currency.

He would place it in the coffin, in lieu of gems,
of silver, of gold and other princessy accoutrements.

Ghost of a Sort

The boy who carries a large wallclock on his back
about-faces the temporary puddle which reflects him.
Time runs backwards in the puddle like the clock's hands.
The boy hasn't yet grown into his nose. He will, once

hormones coax his brows into over-arching his eyes.
When his jaw morphs into the heaviness of an anvil
his face will be a stranger even to himself. His limbs
will ache with growth, his parchment-smooth features

will be pocked by an asteroid-pelting of acne
and folic growth. The grave or cremation kiln the only
alternative. *God forbid*, his mother mouths. Even as she
cherishes his coming gangliness, his shoulders of support,

does she know she will yearn time and time again
to be burdened for a moment or two with the disappeared
child? The boy displaced by a man? We can speculate, her
memory of him as he is now, will be a haunting ghost of a sort.

Stolen

What happened to the two-headed holywater font
carved over twelve hundred years ago, embedded
in a graveyard wall as mere adornment after Proddy

appropriation? Those monkish heads saw William's
Orangeists besiege Elizabeth Fort. Musket balls whined
past their faces then. Over centuries, Croesus-rich

Chattertons paraded their coffins past to their stately tomb.
Philandering couples canoodled beneath the font's
four nostrils when obscured by wild clematis.

How was the smell of pert youth judged by noses
of locally quarried stone? Decades ago I tore back
the undergrowth so the heads could view again

the cloudy/blue skies over Bishop Street and the convent
isle of Saint Maries and how the Ideal Menswear factory
Singered with industry. Now the heads have gone to God

knows where, now when the factory is silent;
when the convent girls are thinning in numbers
widening in girth, and the old nuns no longer shroud

their chaste greying locks with black wimples. Last century
on summer nights with star-riddled skies I slept on a florescence
of untrimmed shoots sprouting four feet tall around the base

of the great elm's bole. The heads adjacent kept the demons
of the surrounding graves at bay; the souls of the never-satisfied
who died well before ready, their names obscured by weathering

on headstones halfsunk from the subsidence of centuries.
The blackbirds trilled their shrill alarm as I awoke and strode
through tall stalks of wild raspberries. But what alarm sounded

when some bastard stole the holywater font with two heads?
Two heads like some underloved, double-headed foetus
sharing one heart? Two heads – my long-missed friends.

Three Months Later

Gently bobbing in the wave-weaved currach
the boy sits with fish-eyed, downward gaze.
It's his first time afloat since his father's drowning.
His village feel his fear of the deep must be
flushed away if ever he's to grow to spread nets
and hooks to harrow the turbulent sea. He dons
a blazer and tie to his father's bobbing gravesite,
curls on his head as tangly as his purling knitwear.

He's held aloft in the currach by the crafted, lopped-
off limbs of a faraway forest. As lumber their tongues
were hewn out. They keen no more of shadowed
ravines and burrowing nocturnal mammals, of how
their berries were once the mountains' periwinkles,
their roosting wood-pigeons mackerel of the skies.

from The State of the Blessed Dead

If grief is a thing with feathers, still it lacks
flight, the feathers, like petrified leaves
of a petrified forest, weighty as a trunk.
When I told them to shorten your suffering

I never meant they should starve and dehydrate
you to death. You rejected the wet sponge
in your mouth, twisted into a rictus
while still alive with eyewhites yellowing.

The fentanyl drip, in the main, pumping to keep
you quiet and manageable. As you worsened
"Oh! you can see the difference now," said
the middle-class *lady* doctors, as proud as of any cake

their mothers might have baked, rising in the oven.
I realised they had never watched somebody die
minute by minute, all day, all week long; in and out
in a jiffy they just glimpsed a soul wisping away.

We live in the State of the Blessed Dead, a polity
where a miracle to be hoped for is nothing as grandiose
as resurrection, but a simple good death, instead of a realm
where the dying shrivel without grace, where the grieving

dread their future. Serenity in such a setting is a worse
kind of derangement than despair. There is no dignity
to a slow death and only a little to slow grief.
"Am I real or what?" your response to my

"What are you thinking?" this, weeks before
when you still had speech, a personality,
before the blast of radium (Dryden's 'heap
of jarring atoms'?) wrenched words away

from you and grunting came on, sounding
like a combustion engine turning over,
in a public ward where men's screams
were tectonic enough to loosen dust

between floorboards. "You're real," said I,
a fabulist, who believes a Realist is one
who conspires to preserve delusions cherished
by the masses. In this moment my mind

has travelled from a future where I can no longer
be *here*, a future where I wish I could still press the warm
flesh of you, smell the unwashed scent of you, listen
to your voice which I heard sing only once, in my distant

childhood, in a house you thought was empty but for you;
a house you thought never listened to your song. I can't
remember your one song, only to never forget
it was something upbeat, something learnt

from Ella or Frank or the Andrews sisters, not Holiday's
'Lover Man Where Have You Gone?' listened by you
one day, over and over in a melancholy funk,
a mystery funk, your wife, my mother, in the next room.

Self-portrait as a Silk Purse

On this shelf lies a small gathering of heirlooms
from four generations. I am the oldest.
Too tiny ever to have held a fortune, my insides

are now smothered with must. Once, my worm-weaved
flesh wrapped dinging copper and silver discs,
loose parts of a prosthetic spine. I'm hardly used.

I never held many coins at once, even pennies,
even old ones, wide as an American half-dollar.
The hens pictured had clinking clucks. My fastening

clasps still open with a crispy click, their bite unworn
from years of snapping shut. Here I await my finding
by a small boy; for him to stash in my stomach

a dinky coin, a cupro-nickel bit sporting a rabbit,
inured to bouncing on many a counter, a thruppence,
pre-decimal, long past the power of purchase.

Self-portrait as 21st Century Frankenstein

The masks on my wall stare down like a dramatic chorus.
A wooden long-chinned Dogon, a dreadlocked Disney Pluto,
a moustachioed plastic *Anonymous* bought online.

All act to lure your gaze from the mask that is my face;
another's face, sewn over my own bones, with muscle
and skin younger than my years. I Lancôme lines on

to make it seem more real, pomade the sheen so my new face
blends better with my neck's looseness. I pocket my two
odd hands, one from a Swede, the other a Spaniard.

One can last longer delving in snow, the other
I can hold closer to the scalding of a flame.
Occasionally I will eye my back in a full-length mirror

and bugle backwards a composition there scored in ink;
bewraying how melodic and booming with sweetness
Anton Webern can sound in reverse. I wonder

about the person who commissioned this tattoo
more than the involuntary donors of my other parts.
I had never heard of Webern before getting my new back.

My left earlobe is longer, more Buddha-like
than my right, and a Star of David is etched there.
The crook of my left elbow is marked by a swastika.

My favourite possession: a pot, part Grecian amphora,
part Ming vase, part Meissen platter, kintsugied together
so that it seems a black-figured hoplite, reaches for a pear

with a hand used to gripping dorata, as if he aims
to throw it at a blue, pagoda-roofed Neuschwanstein.
The whole form's implausible perfection makes me see

how my cracks too are filled with precious material,
if of a parabolic matter, a fact you are empowered
to appraise, once you return your gaze from the masks.

Self-portrait as Half a Sculpture
in the Luxembourg Gardens

Am I simply one who haunts? How long has it been
between breathing, bleeding being and fleshless
occupant of a sveltened stone; smog marks gathering,
green scum spreading between swabbings-down?

Someone's placed a naked shape of woman
in my arms. If this form is occupied by a soul
they haven't yet learned to let me know.
What I would give nowadays for indigestion

or to feel the cold, or aching muscles in my neck.
In winter the wind whisks a threnody
from my whitened crown. I watch couples
tread the pathways, pausing to look at me,

comparing themselves in the early days
of their lives, of their romance, to the sculptor's
chiselling of an ideal. Am I here as punishment?
How have I synapseless thoughts?

And does the one who put me here hear
me now, above the musings of a million others
trapped in stones and trees, in the swirl
of a river's flow, the leaf-bashing of a breeze?

Self-portrait at Sixteen

December sixteenth 1979, I came across
the headstone of Sarah Paddington who departed
this life aged sixteen on December sixteenth 1821.

A grey slab laid flat, its incisions legible
only on a rainy day, since the inclemency
of decades had worn rough its limestone surface

once polished and crisp but now blotched
with segments of exposed crinoids old
by as many years as there are raindrops

in a province-wide storm. That day's rain
had eased. The gargoyle gutter spouts
gargled to a glugging halt. I was strolling

in the grounds of St. Fin Barre's cathedral
sixteen years old myself and speculated
no one had thought of Sarah Paddington

in a century, not even the workmen
who had moved her headstone, too busy to read it
when the rebuilt cathedral spread out sixty years

after she had gone in the ground. Beneath my boots
lichen slithered a million times slower than snails.
I reckoned the soul of Sarah Paddington had summoned

me to her headstone on her anniversary.
Sceptics will snigger over magical thinking
but I could only believe Miss Paddington wanted

someone to think of her, to imagine her
in a Fitton Street parlour with blonde ringlets,
regaled in a flouncing party dress, blue eyes

coached to be coquettish at men older than me
before whatever pestilence wasted her so young,
entered her and thinned her to a breathless stick.

Later I lit a candle for her Purgatory-dwelling
Protestant heart, at Catholic St. Augustine's.

NOTES

p.14 in 'Doll Maker', *seanaithir* is Irish for grandfather

p.17 in 'Filial Duty' sconcing – to sconce, as verb, is Hiberno-English dialect for to visually-examine closely and quickly.

p.30 'Louse Float Daze' is composed of altered locutions and lines from John Ashbury's book *Houseboat Days*.

P. 35 the "it" found and kept by Gallagher's brother as reported in *Union of Catholic Asian News,* was one of the stone angel heads.